Our Global Community

Games

Lisa Easterling

www.heinemann.co.uk/library
Visit our website to find out more information about Heinemann Library books.

To order:
☎ Phone 44 (0) 1865 888066
Send a fax to 44 (0) 1865 314091
📄 Visit the Heinemann Bookshop at www.heinemann.co.uk/library to browse our
 catalogue and order online.

First published in Great Britain by Heinemann Library, Halley Court, Jordan Hill, Oxford OX2 8EJ, part of Harcourt Education. Heinemann is a registered trademark of Harcourt Education Ltd.

© Harcourt Education Ltd 2007
First published in paperback in 2008
The moral right of the proprietor has been asserted.

Editorial: Diyan Leake
Design: Joanna Hinton-Malivoire
Picture research: Ruth Smith
Production: Duncan Gilbert

Origination: Chroma Graphics (Overseas) Pte Ltd
Printed and bound in China by South China Printing Company Ltd

ISBN 978 0 431 19106 5 (hardback)
11 10 09 08 07
10 9 8 7 6 5 4 3 2 1

ISBN 978 0 431 19115 7 (paperback)
12 11 10 09 08
10 9 8 7 6 5 4 3 2 1

British Library Cataloguing in Publication Data
Easterling, Lisa
Games. - (Our global community)
1. Games - Juvenile literature
I. Title
306.4'87

Acknowledgements
The publishers would like to thank the following for permission to reproduce photographs: Alamy pp. **8** (Danita Delimont), **9** (Robert Fried), **12** (Huw Jones), **15** (Kevin Foy), **19** (Ingram Publishing); Corbis pp. **4** (David H Wells); **7** (Nik Wheeler), **11** (Tom Stewart), **14** (Annie Griffiths Belt), **17** (Ronnie Kaufman), **17** (Jack Fields), **20**, **23** (Nik Wheeler; Jack Fields); Getty Images pp. **5** (Stone), **6** (Reportage), **10** (Imagebank), **13** (Photodisc Green); Jupiter Images p. **16** (Dynamic Graphics).

Cover photograph of boys playing marbles reproduced with permission of Alamy/Ace Stock Ltd.

Every effort has been made to contact copyright holders of any material reproduced in this book. Any omissions will be rectified in subsequent printings if notice is given to the publishers.

Contents

Games around the world

All around the world, people play games.

People play games for fun.

Games are different from place
to place.

All games have rules.

Types of games

Some games are played alone.

Some games are played with
other people.

People play games with cards.

Snap is a card game.

Some people like to play with a
yo-yo on a string.

Some people like to play Cat's Cradle with string.

Some games are played with balls.

Football is a ball game.

Some games are played on a board.

Chess is a board game.

Some games are played on
the pavement.

Hopscotch is played on the pavement.

It is fun to play games.

What games do you like to play?

How to play Hopscotch

1. Draw a Hopscotch board. (See page 19.)
2. Throw a pebble on to Square 1.
3. Hop over that square.
4. Hop and jump to the top of the board and back again.
5. When you hop back to Square 2, pick up the pebble from Square 1.
6. Do this for all the squares.

Hopscotch rules

1. The pebble must land in the correct square.
2. You must not step on the Hopscotch lines.
3. You can only put one foot in each square.

Picture glossary

pavement hard surface you can walk on. You can play games on a pavement.

rule something that you must follow. Games have rules.

Index

Notes for parents and teachers

Before reading

Talk to the children about games. Ask them what their favourite games are. Ask them if they like playing in groups of two or in larger groups. What games can they think of that need only two players? What games are played in teams? Ask them to think about the rules of a team game. Why do they think rules are important? Explain that games are played all over the world. Some games are very similar but the rules might be a little different.

After reading

Favourite games. Make a list of the games that the children say they like playing. Ask them to vote for their favourite game. If possible, arrange for the group to play this game.

Snap. Talk to the children about playing Snap. Divide the children into pairs and give each pair 20 cards. There should be four cards that match so that the Snap situation occurs frequently. Talk about the rules of the game and demonstrate how to play the game. Then encourage the children to work with a partner and to play Snap.

A new game. Ask the children to help you to make up a new playground game with teams. Explain that there are two teams and they must try to get a ball across the playground without touching the ground. Discuss with them the rules of this new game. When they are clear about the rules, play the game.